BLOOM

AND

LACERATION

BLOOM
AND
LACERATION

—— *poems* ——

RALPH BLACK

GREEN WRITERS PRESS *Brattleboro, Vermont*

Printed in the United States

10 9 8 7 6 5 4 3 2 1

Green Writers Press is a Vermont-based publisher whose mission is to spread a message of hope and renewal through the words and images we publish. Throughout we will adhere to our commitment to preserving and protecting the natural resources of the earth. To that end, a percentage of our proceeds will be donated to environmental activist groups. Green Writers Press gratefully acknowledges support from individual donors, friends, and readers to help support the environment and our publishing initiative.

gReen
wriTers
press

Giving Voice to Writers & Artists Who Will Make the World a Better Place
Green Writers Press | Brattleboro, Vermont
www.greenwriterspress.com

ISBN: 978-0-9994995-7-3

COVER: DESIGNED BY HANNAH WOOD
COVER ART:
Albrecht Dürer, "Wing of a European Roller,"
watercolor, 19.6 x 20 centimeters,
from the collection of the Albertina, Vienna.

PRINTED ON RECYCLED PAPER BY BOOKMOBILE.
BASED IN MINNEAPOLIS, MINNESOTA, BOOKMOBILE BEGAN AS A DESIGN AND TYPESETTING PRODUCTION HOUSE IN 1982 AND STARTED OFFERING PRINT SERVICES IN 1996. BOOKMOBILE IS RUN ON 100% WIND- AND SOLAR-POWERED CLEAN ENERGY.

CONTENTS

This shaking keeps me steady. I should know.
What falls away is always. And is near.

—THEODORE ROETHKE

For Susan, Anna, and Elise

ONE

21ST CENTURY LECTURE

Listen. You know what a torn shirt
the world's become. You know how thin
its fabric. You know what seams are,
and how your life, as though by accident,
settles in and trembles them apart.
And everyone knows you don't mean it.
So you say to yourself, don't be stupid.
You say, don't sham and swindle your way
through these stark desecrations,
don't stand around as your body's
warming waters rise, as they lift
and pool around the trunks
of three hundred year old trees—
the ones that snatched away your breath
and all your words when you were a kid.
Your tea is getting cold. The shirts
you bought on a whim have to go back
to the Singapore sweatshop.
You're smart and caring enough, muttering
over the paper each morning,
tuned in to just the right litany of fear—
Bagdad, Darfur, the Bronx—
the outstretched or instantly severed hand.
You could turn the page from the steady
unraveling of the planet's bright threads.
But your throat rasps and freezes at the sight
of the sea lion sow chewing the face
off her newborn pup; at the Coho hatchlings
spilling out of the hatchery flume,
carrying their constellations of DNA

up and against the river's age-old equations;
at the polar bears starving at the edge
of their ice. You know the word *starving*,
you know the meaning of CO_2, you know
how apple seeds and smart bombs bloom,
how simple it is to flay a range of hills,
eviscerate a mountain with a spark.
You know how the stones can keep you warm.
You're not an idiot. You're not a fool.
You won't let your heart, that tiny,
glacial island, fracture and calve.
You think your love for your children
and your children's love for everything
but homework and spinach should be plenty.
The name of the wind is changing.
The wind, which you know is your breath,
and spills over flooded deltas, which churns
through the gleaming thickets of oil refineries,
fission factories, wind farms, water mills,
think tanks, smelters, grinders, brothels,
landfills, gun shops, billboards declaring
the newest-brightest-best—you know
how it fills you, how it lifts away from you
the words you use to talk back to yourself
late into the night. It's a very old wind, and you
utter it over and over, part mantra, part koan,
a playing-out of words like an old uncle spiraling
ten-pound test over his favorite run of rapids
thirty miles up the East Fork of that river
that spills now green and empty as an eye.
You know all this. No one's telling you anything
you haven't known for a hundred years.
But your tongue says *say it*, just the same.

Your mouth makes the shape of a call, a cry,
an uneven song. You reach for a pen,
tired as you are. You write it down, because
stories and maps are the same. You think
of the photograph you saw at the museum:
a ten year old boy born blind who lost
both his arms in his country's war.
He's at a desk, reading a book with his mouth.
He's leaning in and kissing the words,
in love with his own hunger.
He's doing with his whole body
everything he knows how to do.

BUDDHAHOOD

Release the world's bright strings, go the musings
    of the Buddha, fraying parchment
        and the dust of words. A man sits for forty-nine days

by a mud-washed river, never once complaining
    of the ants tangled in the hairs
        of his arms, or of mayflies sipping salt water

from the unsleeping corners of his eyes. Me?
    Most days I sit in a thrift store armchair,
        blinking my way into the sweet delirium

of maple and ash, fleeting, sequined worlds
    streaming across the mossy caves of consciousness.
        My head is swathed in veils that are swathed

in veils, silken and muffling. When I get outside
    I like to sit on the weed-choked lawn,
        cross-legged, oblivious as a child.

I like the sun at my back, my shadow inching forward
    like spilled ink, foraging
        toward darkness. The afternoon swirls

with loam-rot and yesterday's rain.
    Dragonflies stitch the light, scalpel-winged
    and fully awake.

While I, while I—I twine my fingers
        into the frayed ropes of the grasses, holding on tight
        to where I belong.

Swimming Lesson

Go ahead hungry monk, strip down
to your Speedos, wade to your unglamorized ankles
into April's needling surf, those tiny,
scavenging waves the Master parabled against:
so many mouths in the world, so little kissing.
Leave your prayer flags bannering like anemones
on the beach. Forget the cities of alabaster
and mud chiseled into the mountain's high relief.
Let drift the chaff of the evening gong,
the morning's bowl of tea, thin and green as celadon.
Think of something like heaven as your body's
lifted, as it's held almost in place by fingerlings
of light, bones worn on the outside delicate
as diatoms. The sun on your back will atomize
your scheming cells, the cold water drizzling
into the crack between mask and grimace will leave
on your cheeks its thousand drying stars, a galaxy
of salt. Go on, flippering novice, suck down
through the snorkel that thick bubble of air,
a shimmering weight tied to a drowned thread,
then kick even deeper into the unsounded blue,
counting as you descend the starfish suctioned
to their ephemeral rocks, and the jellyfish, those
precarious dreams drifting past, reaching out to you
their tendrilled, intoxicating songs.

APIARIAL

My daughter can't sleep
    for the vanishing bees. She slumps

down the stairs dazed
    as a sleepwalker, a stargazer

trailing a swarm of bad dreams.
    She drifts without moving into

the moon-slatted light
    of the sloping yard. She can't sleep

as the bees disappear from
    the pecan groves of Georgia, from

the blackberry fields of Maine,
    from the pear orchards of central China.

She turns from vibrating dreams
    of bee-shadows and bee-shrouds,

as scientists parse the broken-down
    machinery of bees, small children

in their front yards looping
    endless chains of clover. Until

the bees reappear, lining up
    along the branches of the linden, her

story-laden tree. They park there,
    fifty on one branch, a hundred

on another, a fleet of tiny busses
    idling into the future. She knows

about compound eyes, their
    seven-thousand hexagonal lenses.

She knows how those gilded windows
    help orchestrate the light:

a thousand shifting facets, a million
    maps danced into the air.

The night is filled with zithering,
    and a girl who carries inside her

the violet hum of meadows,
    a steady, quickening blur.

SLEIGHT OF HAND

Most nights after dinner
my mother would drop the needle
of the living room stereo
onto just the right groove
of the record, knowing which tune
would lull the small boats of our bodies
toward sleep. Sometimes,
if she'd downed too many vodkas
from the stashed jug in her closet,
the needle would skitter across the disk
like a storm of insects, settling
like the quiet after a car crash
into Mozart or Bach, as though
we'd been there all along, nothing
amiss, not Horowitz's allegro, not
Gould's hummed andante—the music
riding us along the long peninsula
of sleep. She swayed with a kind of magic,
the miniature wand of her cigarette
signaling degree, my mother
in her black dress and amber pendant,
casting secrets through the house.
Just as, months later, we stood
at an overlook in the Blue Ridge
mountains, our sandwiches finished,
the sun drifting like a brushstroke
across the valley. And there,
framed in the bloodshot afterglow
of afternoon, when each of us was
thinking about anything else, she lifted

a rock from the rock wall we were
leaning against, revealing with a tremulous
wave of her hand the ten-thousand
ladybugs that somehow had been herded
into the crushed black space
between shadow and stone.
They teetered about drunkenly
in the sudden eruption of daylight,
as we all did standing there, watching
as one by one the insects flurried up
into the valley, drifting, breaking apart,
letting the current take them.

READING KEATS IN OCTOBER

October's red sun on October's red leaves—
 cauterized, redundant. Miles of this,
modal, the way Keats once tuned
 his iPod to *Kind of Blue*, then scrolled
to "Flamenco Sketches"—the perfect tune
 for a latte on the Spanish Steps,
cold as it was, coughing up spherules of blood.
 Part of the mood is the leaky
fountain, the dwindling boat
 a miniscule drumming. Water that scatters
the *luce l'autunno* of Rome.
 To do this right, to get it, as the painters say,
just so, you'd have to crack open
 half a dozen acrylics tubes—
a murmurous blue, a delirium ochre,
 a yellow like rained-on sunflowers.
You'd have to ask the locals
 for the name of the color of the hills
in the hour when afternoon washes
 into dark. That name. The French
would know how to parse the word
 for just the right tone or shade,
the way Proust knew how to tune
 a room for story, or Marcel Marceau
(gods of silence, bless his hands) knew
 the body's fluid Braille. Move
and speak. Move and speak. The way ash
 and red oak do. The way John Keats did
those last months of zeroing in
 on autumn's chromatic cues—

thatch-tone and hazel-note. He is dying
    all over again, practicing words like
fume and *ooze* and *sallow*. He is all
    bruise and laceration, but the words
for the season are sharp on his tongue.

AFTER ALL

The morning isn't a riddle
after all, but a problem,
an unfigured sum, digits climbing,

decimals moving up the row,
zeros speaking their open-throated
songs of praise.

The afternoon isn't, after all,
a shepherd napping on a hill,
but a Rabbi wide awake on a bench

on a boulevard of sycamores—
two or three worlds away
from where I sit, on another bench,

watching a row of blackbirds
clatter along a wire like abacus beads,
tallying with Gnostic zeal.

Even the evening
isn't evening after all, but
something less, dusk

subtracted from dark, the moon's
remainder pared down, carried over
to the next sliver of dawn,

where a few stars languish
like tarnished coins,
and snails glister over wet leaves,

where the day's ledger lies open
on a table, all but unreadable
in this thinning parchment of light.

LOOK UP

The name of the tree
with no leaves on the slight rise
above the pond,

the name of the back-lit
silhouetted bird chirring from
one of its branches,

and then the name for the patches
of air transposed by the bird's
unanticipated lift. Look up

the name for the unhurried
stride of the man in the blue canvas jacket
walking just then down the road,

and also the name of the angle
his hand makes tilted
above his eyes as he watches

the blur of what must be
the bird, a streak now, an arc
of total diminishment.

And don't forget the name
for the spot halfway exactly
between the man and the limb-

from-which-the-bird-has-flown,
which is, as Plato said,
    the spiraled core of seeing—

    the triangulated country
where the sun shines down
    and reflects out from

    the man's squinted eyes
and from the fading iridescence
    of the bird.

    The world, the prophets say,
is made of mirrors, shards of light
    strewn like riddles along

    the murky path. You look up
from where you are
    and find yourself caught

    in the flash of a tree root
or snow bank, the day a wave
    of fractalling weather.

    A yellow leaf stutters
at the fiery tip of a maple branch
    a moment before a cold wind

    turns, suddenly as this, and
tumbles it away. Leaving you
    standing there, eye-deep

in the place you've always been,
the day like fistfuls of water
dwindling through your fingers.

Brown Pelican, East Grand Terre Island, Louisiana, June, 2010

after a photograph by Charlie Reidel

What if, after all, he is
what he appears to be,

a huge clambering bird,
unliftable now, a wrecked god

caught in the tarred lungs
of the planet? What if

what appears to be happening
is happening, pixels

on a screen dissolve to an
actual death, Zeusian creature

being shuddered in two
and two again,

because of air and water,
because of dirt and injured light,

elements that were, till this
very moment, home.

His head is raised, archaic
beak gaped in rasped exclamation,

wings combustible
with the extrusion of rocks,

with a knowledge of a hunger
even he in his dying

does not understand. Atoms
converge and blacken, explode

like seed pods. Syllables hinge
and rust, swinging

on stories we tell ourselves
about a further field. What if,

as the stones begin to burn
we forget the thrum of those great,

still-beating wings? Something
is torn from the sky's

bright fabric, a bead of light
shuttered like a sutured eye.

Self-Portrait in Winter

The snow keeps pouring like God's own blindness
out of the tintype sky. A truck gears down
at the top of the hill, gray-tones
bleeding into sepia.

You know already how this
is going to end, a slow-motion newsreel
clattering along, then the misaligned sprockets,
the calamity sputtering in place.

My questions are simple: am I the man
in the truck tuning through the static
for a hummable song? or the kid by the underpass,
pressing pebbles into snowballs,
fashioning a pile?

Am I the deer, a large doe, browsing
at the edge of the understoried woods, or the hunter
camo'd against the trunk of an oak,
nestling the gunstock into his shoulder?

The snow is horizontal now, the afternoon
scored like old glass. A man in quilted coveralls
steps into the frame. He's peering over a chin-high armload
    of wood.
He's entered the pattern, part of the symmetry

settling into place. Though he's stopped now
and is turning toward the slight angle of roofline
just visible at the hill's blowsy cusp.

It might be the wind he hears, or a voice
caught and transmuted by wind, a ringing
somewhere between song and lamentation.

The truck is halfway down the mountain,
the story almost done. All the players
in position, the scenery flocked in diffusing light.

I am calling to the boy to stay down,
to the truck driver to please just this once
look up from the dial's mesmerizing glow.

The deer twitches at nothing, lifts her front leg, holds it
urgently still. The hunter sucks a fistful of cold
into his lungs, steadies a bead along the sight-line.

There is always a trigger. There is always
a page to turn.

Because I Do Not Play the Cello

I'm partial to the crepuscular,
a slow diminuendo of light
over a landscape I have only just begun
to know. Evening, then, and I walk
along the cliff-edge, the grass
almost to my knees, the gorse still wet
with rain. I am humming a little dirge
as I go, dragging my feet a little,
rolling a little pebble around
in my mouth. A small music, perhaps,
a tinny, vibratoless tune that
lets me sound this echoing, human chamber.
The crows have disappeared,
though the gray wake of their going
stirs through still and sharpens the air.
There are hours for such walking,
a kind of disappearance that assembles
ensembles: sonata for unaccompanied
stillness, *allegro, ma non troppo.*
Later, at home, the fire sinks low
into the grate, and my wife, still sleeping,
rolls toward my open hands—
a body at rest in motion, a ravenous
tuning toward perfect pitch.
Curve by curvature, I learn to love
the cellist's tremulous art, the purfled body
of maple and spruce swelling with song.
The way Maestro Rostropovich,
hearing again the bird-brimmed choruses
of a Moscow spring, conjured

a torrent of notes from the tonewood,
a plume of sound lifting like a flock
of startled thrushes. Or how Casals,
rehearsing once on the emptied stage
of Carnegie Hall, dreamt of avocado orchards
in southern Spain, his left hand tremolling
the sweet sarabande of Bach's second suite in D.
The sky is the color of pencil-lead,
the neighborhood cats are ghosting
through the trees, murling their plaintive notes
to listeners who lean against the trunks,
dreaming in the key of cello-wood,
weeping at a sound only the moon should make.
Rain is falling again, and the sea is rising
on the strand, a huge blue curtain
drawing itself over the rocks.
I know what they say about music,
how the bones can vibrate like varnished wood;
how the hands, curled for crescendo,
can gather a few notes from the air,
but never, not ever hold them for long.
I know that the cello is not a boat.
But I am out here regardless,
kneeling lightly on the hull,
rosining the bow before I oar it
for all I'm worth
out into the lifting waves.

TWO

EITHER/OR

A good day for an altar.
A good day for watching the weather.

At the granite kitchen counter, the teenager
pauses between the apple and the pear.

The pitcher eyes the batter,
considers a curve, then rifles a slider.

The cormorant's dive is pure hunger.
The pelican's giddy with humor.

The wind meets the trees with a clatter.
The kid hunched in his treehouse hears a whisper.

The crumbled sky tugs at its tether.
The rocks grip down, knowing nothing better.

A boy scooters by a convenience store.
An old man flicks his smoke before starting his car.

Who will tell the mother about her son, the soldier—
his thin shirt of fear, and not enough armor?

Deeper toward the reef kicks the diver,
hauling his capsule of air through a galaxy of water.

How easily the earth is torn—like frayed sheets, like paper.
Whose body will bandage it back? Whose thread will suture?

The monk sweeps the temple floor.
The soldiers clean their rifles in the square.

A girl brushing her hair before her mirror,
glimpses herself, a stranger, vanishing around the corner.

Back at the altar, the novice at prayer.
Back at the tavern, the barman pours.

In the voting booth the voter
considers each lever, flicks a trigger.

The sun remembers its cousins the stars.
The gardener digs in a row of asters.

What does the granite say to the sculptor?
Or sculptor to stone, with chisel and hammer?

The surgeon cuts into the patient's aorta—
one quavering heart kick-starting another.

Every sea rhymes with every shore.
Every stone with every wing conspires.

GAMES THAT CROWS PLAY

Steal the foil.
    Hide the bauble.
        Tease the tether.
            Spin the pinwheel.

Dust the blackboard.
    Lean on shadows.
        Smear the smokescreen.
            Shade the windows.

Squinch the squeezebox.
    Strut the banjo.
        Swing the night air.
            Waltz the tango.

Buzz the moonlight.
    Chirr at midnight.
        Clack the daylight.
            Kiss it goodnight.

Coo at weathervanes.
    Cluck at windowpanes.
        Caw at thunderstorms.
            Squawk your own name.

Freeze the sun glare.
    Melt the snow globe.
        Surf the spring-melt.
            Hop the leaf-loam.

Peck the bongos.
    Plink pianos.
        Scratch out ragtime.
            Blow the crow blues.

Zip up breezes.
    Knock down hail stones.
        Pester snowflakes.
            Prop up old bones.

Glean the carcass.
    Strip the sinew.
        Nip the bone-sack.
            Groove the new you.

Climb the beanstalk.
    Jab the Jabberwock.
        Jump the candlestick.
            Flee the flooded ark.

Loose the doorjambs.
    Slant the lightning.
        Dim the demigod.
            Crimp the crooked thing.

Crave the raven.
    Shine the grackle.
        Blush the blackbird.
            Scare the scarecrow.

Point the pencil.
    Dip the paintbrush.
        Toss the paper.
            Let the words come.

GARLAND OF BEARS

Wouldn't it be great
to write nothing at all
except poems about bears?

—HAYDEN CARRUTH

I.

A morning like ice at the ice-fringed window,
a mug of cooling coffee in my hand.
On the snow-clumped sidewalk, a boy leads
a black bear with a rope, just a boy and a bear walking.
Every day, three or four dreams awaken
into the world, amble along. And sometimes
you look up and recognize that place: The bear's
bright collar laced with small bells, its muzzle
a mesh of tooled leather. Small wreaths
of snow whisper around both their heads.

2.

It's only half a mile
up the creek, back behind
the listing barn, where
the drenched sack of smashed apples
and week-old chicken
swings from a low branch.

On a plywood platform
in the tree across the creek,
a man dozes in his parka,
blue as his own shadow.
His rifle is balanced
on his lap like a trophy,
polished like a cherished bruise.

He'll be wakened
by a shifting in the air,
by the morning's grunt
of hunger, a gravelly breath
huffed out. He'll aim
as he always aims,
inhaling once, holding
the moment steady, then
squeezing the daylights
out of the day.

3.

I remember the bicycle,
which was red, and the frilly
Renaissance collar he wore,
a crumpled yellow. I remember
sitting with my father and brothers
in the stands, watching this bear,
a large cub pedaling the tricycle
around the ring, while the man
in the coattails and black fedora
called to the rustling crowd: *See here
the world's only bicycling bear,*
while his whip snapped just above
the bear's tufted head.
I doubt that I turned away,
though I'm sure I blinked, perhaps
with amazement, given my age,
with trying to see some figure
other than myself in the dingy mirror
the world dangled before me.
I like to think I tasted something,
young as I was, of human cruelty,
how it drapes itself in such
bright spangles, how it calls to us
to lean in close, to take in
enthrallment's captivating show.

4.

During the siege of my city,
the snipers in Sniper's Alley
picked off men and women
scurrying across town for a jug
of water, a loaf of bread—
the ones who couldn't flee.
Sometimes a white flag
would appear, fluttering at the corner
of a building before the head
and body of the runner, and sometimes
the snipers would let them pass.
It was uncomplicated work, and some
kept bottles of vodka or scotch,
and cartons of imported cigarettes
to help with the plodding days.

But when the animals escaped
from the Municipal Zoo,
led by hunger through the city,
word went out among
the shooters outposted in
abandoned bedrooms and dens.
Bets were laid, bounties
posted: this much for a bison,
this much for an elk or badger.
The highest prices went for
the bears who came like the dreams
of forgotten relatives wobbling
down the street, pursued
by their own hunger.

Sometimes the bears looked
like old women hunched
over cooking pots, and sometimes
like nothing but bears
trundling darkly out of the stars,
as though the sky had been
tipped on its side, a thousand
ragged constellations
spilling onto the streets.

5.

Then somewhere
there was one, then
where the last one was
was a bear-shaped blank
in the forest, a stencil
of bear where the trees
had been, where the bear
had uncurled itself
from bear frond
and bear pod, bear seed
or seam of bear quartz
crashing through
granite and the wind
carried a not quite scent,
a tremor perhaps,
a small upending
undersong of bear
that no one wandering
this way would mistake
for what had been.

6.

I am five, maybe six,
I am naked as a cub
and stepping into my mother's
fur coat, the muffling weight
of thick animal: wolverine,
coyote, panther, mink.
I am the glass-eyed bear,
the red-stitched crooked mouth
that keeps quiet quietly propped
against a pillow, I am the pillow
stuffed with a life that
once and not so long ago—
I read it in a book—padded
through the cooling shadows
of tamarack and willow,
wandering to the fern-thick
rill of creek bottom,
digging at roots, snuffling
the rot of new growth, then
vanishing into the absolute
stillness of my mother
standing for how many minutes
at the door, looming there
in all her squinted curiosity,
leveling at me her practiced
skeptical gaze, and her grin.

7.

You could almost see him
through the interlapping light
pouring over the fence,
shambling to the feeder,
tearing it from a branch
and rocking back then
on haunches wide as dusk
to snack on sunflower hulls
and millet hearts, chewing
through globs of suet, though
this time I'm almost sure
the shape that cast all that shadow,
that squinted and sniffed
at the knitted air was more and
also less than what might be
imagined, the way night's riffling cape
shifts between glimpse and gone
and you can taste it—can you
taste it?—a metallic edge
to the tongue, a half-brother
returning from distant wars,
a drunken uncle trying
one more time to steady
the world's unseemly wobble,
a father returned to the backyard
of his very own house, fattening himself
on morsels and scraps, ravenous
and wary in his blackened,
rummaged clothes.

8.

In every poem of Whitman's
a bear: summer bears
drunk on the berries
of Central Park,
autumn bears bustling
into a tavern near
the docks, knocking over
chairs, having a time.
And one walking along
the weedy edge of Antietam
or Fredericksburg, wagging
his head from side to side,
something like smoke
blowing through his fur.

In every poem of Dickinson's
the passage of bears:
the passing through,
the just disappearing of bear
through the hedgerow,
the bramble, through the
garden's daylilies and trillium
where you can still, through
the scrim, see them going.
And one on the path
in front of the house,
the size of a bee, of a star,
shimmery in moonlight
just visible from
the bedroom window.

9.

for Hayden Carruth

The worn, gray poet urges himself
out of a chair, long Sasquatch beard,
hair a sheaf of blown straw.
He half leans on, half pulls along
a canister of air, the clear tube looping
up to his nose, parceling the breath,
sip by sip, sweet as honeysuckle.

Old bear, old poet, looking up from the podium
at the young, startled faces, hanging on
to thickets of words, following
the mechanical breath, saying your
many-berried, bear-scatted poems, flecks
of pine bark, hay grit, roof tar, how
they bear the cumbersome weight of
all that love, all that longing, a daily blues—
a grizzly blowing wild on a tenor sax.

One poem a snow shovel's
laden weight, one poem an egret feather
woozy in an updraft. And one
nothing but scent, pure lyric odor
blowing in from somewhere
no one in the room can quite place.

10.

At the end of the driveway
the back side of a black bear
disappears into the woods.
I lift my hand as if to say
stay a while, tell me
who you are. But he knows
the shoulds and oughts
of the open hand, what blundering
language his clever,
upright brethren have learned
from the stones they used
to turn, the roots devour.
So he pours himself back
into the cave of the woods,
leaving me with a hand
in the air, empty, full of questions,
taking in the noise
of the uncomplicated rain.

THREE

THAW

The dulled edge of March and the city is a fist,
    blunt, tightly gripped, winter caving in
a little more each day. And the people waking
    and moving through the city are themselves
a species of fist, coiled like shells, ropey,
    levered into a horizontal threshing of wind.
They know that spring is a tiny, unrustable seed,
    a protozoan something, raw with origin, clenched
even now in their thickly-gloved hands. They believe
    in its fierce pliability, a tidbit of redemption,
like some Megaraptor spore frozen for eighty,
    maybe ninety million years in Siberian tundra,
then nuked by a rogue, disenchanted Bolshevik,
    thawed and fed with radioactive stew, and half
of Moscow tumbles. It's a lesson the Soviets learned
    long ago, how White Nights give way to cool,
sky-domed summer avenues, drowsed with willows
    and the Czar's beloved oaks. It's why, at the tattered
end of winter, you sometimes see three or four kids,
    sixth or seventh grade boys, kick-starting their way
home from school. Why they stop, sometimes,
    at the largest maple on the block, a yard-busting,
wind-shearing mother of a tree. They're not so old
    to have forgotten wonder, or so young they haven't
learned to distinguish dirt from dream, element
    from the siren song of myth. So they look up
into the sprawled, skeletal branches and then,
    as though they'd rehearsed for days, join hands
and circle the tree, their cheeks imprinted
    with the Mesozoic topography of the trunk.

Perhaps they've read in school about the layer
    just below the pebbled bark that moves the juices up
from the roots, and what they want is to hug
    some warmth back into the bole of that old beauty.
Or maybe they're tired of waiting for bud-tip
    and leaf-curl to flute open, hell-bent on squeezing
the bejesus out of the granddaddy maple, strangling back
    into it some green-flumed action. As for the tree itself
and the faint possibility of arboreal reciprocation,
    no one sees the flecks of mapley DNA sifting into
the cheek pores and palm lines of the circled boys.
    It'll takes some years before they feel the phloem-like
cellular tug, a reed-thin trilling in their veins.
    A man hard-raking the blanched winter grass
from his lawn, kicking away the few last turds
    of snow from under the boxwoods, watches
the kids unlink, regroup, sees them look up
    one more time into the crazed geometry
of the tree, then head off down the road.
    Nothing to it, he thinks, or not much
to joining the ends of two seasons together,
    seeing the body for what it is, a fulcrum,
a wire, a flesh and bone winch rolled out
    into the yard a few times each year,
put to work. It's fractal and wild as ice,
    a bit of chaos theory detheorized, laid bare—
a fossilized fern leaf unfurling from stone.
    A woman walking her mutt of a dog watches
the man leaning on his rake, wagging his head
    at something she's missed. She's glad to see
someone else outside, someone broken free
    or breaking, someone unknotting out here
beneath the sun's smeared thumbprint,
    tiny birds ribboning from his half-open mouth.

Apple Psalm

My new god is the apple seed,
that dim, black, spitoutable being.

Not the apple or the apple tree, though
those'll come, if you let them.

Only the seed, with the roots and bole,
the wind-wracked limbs packed into it,

the core of daylight burning there,
ready to split its slick red jacket.

I love to bobble my god around
from hand to hand, to hold him a while

on my tongue. I love to carry him,
light as a prayer in my shirt pocket,

as I walk to the market for a piece
of fruit. How happy I am in this glow

of certainty, reciting the faithful prayers
of the apple, the apple psalms,

the parables of the burgeoning globe.
How pleased, bowing down to the tiny seed,

to press him with my finger deep
into the resuscitating dirt.

GREAT BLUE

The way he flaps down into the yard,
this gray spindled kite, dragging
a length of shadow behind him,
Pleistocenean angel, hungered by all the years
of his absence for the darting koi
in our tub-sized pond.

We watch him from our breakfast table,
strewn as usual with cereal bowls and cold toast,
as he heaves those half-broken shoulders
down through the trees, and lands,
or rather crash-falls on the rocks
by the water's reedy edge.

And the rest of us, we stand
at the breath-fogged window, mouthing
forgotten alphabets, another American family
rung full by this grand visitation—
breakfast spoons and butter knives in hand,
floral PJs hoisted up, as though company had come
and we'd just put on our finery.

My daughters started jigging
right there in the kitchen, kicking up their knees
and flailing their small arms,
as though pithed by a hot shard.
I'd seen it before, the way the world
sneaks up and up-ends them,
the way light flashes into them,
or some creature spied at the top of a hill
fissures right down into their bones.

Once my daughter, only ten-months old,
followed the shine of a copper beetle
from our stooped front step to the horse farm
at the county line. And then, years later,
her sister, not much more than two,
climbed thirty feet into a tulip poplar.
We found her dozing in the rooted tangle
of a squirrel's nest, fists clenched with acorn caps,
hair tufted up and streaked with gray.

And when they vanish
quick as a held breath from the room
no one is surprised. And when they appear
like a sharp breath released, leaping
across the lawn, flapping their
pale arms past the reddening maple
and the stir of rhododendron,
all we can do is nod at the bright
transformation:

                    These two,
so recently my daughters,
returning to the mother-cry of flight,
their shoulders hunched and twitching
as the heron hops back into the sky
and the grass lifts and lifts them
into another ordinary day.

PORTRAIT OF MY DAUGHTER AS A YOUNG BUDDHA

Maybe it's the way she sits
at the dinner table, legs tucked beneath her,
beaming fully at her plate, as though
the heap of fettuccini bolognaise was nothing
but an edible mandala, an eight-fold
al-dente koan that will lead her
to the sated side of emptiness.

Or how some mornings, still pink
from the shower's stuttering jets, she kneels
on her bed, wrapped and enrapt
in a large gold towel, back straight, head tipped
high as a lotus, one arm curved across
the universe of her belly.

I've seen her pour buckets of sand
into the ocean, dump seawater onto temples
of sand, sluicing the ephemeral into
the eternal as though both were pieces
in a child's game. I've heard her cry out at night
a sound like wind oming through a grove
of aspen, then wake on the ragged border of sleep,
her eyes enjewelled with a glimpse
brought back from fleeting worlds.

So I call her who she is: Gautama,
Saugata, Bodihisattva, Elise, a four-chant name
I repeat like a mantra, hoping to reach her
in the dharma-swirled practice
of morning cartoons.

The way she berates her sister
for breathing, or leaves socks in the fruit bowl
at night, the way she holds in her body
a vortex of noise, releasing it
like a previous incarnation—a fleet-footed,
night-nosing, kink-tailed caterwaul—might lead some
to doubt the nature of her true nature.

But she knows every song is a sutra,
every road a way out and back in. She knows
what a stone means meeting water,
and what a bell sounds like
the moment before it is struck.

THE ART OF STONE

I am glad for the rain silvering the stones,
    and for the three pendulous notes of the thrush
        repeating a small blues over and over,
even though the day is cracked jade.
    And for the stone masons from Krakow,
        the father in his straw hat and constant
cigarette, the son who does the talking, shuttling
    between his decent English and lousy French
        like a plumb-bob, a tipsy level,
returning each time to some flecked syllable
    of Polish, sounding for a moment like what I think
        a snippet from a Milosz poem might sound like.
I am glad to think, even wrongly, of Milosz
    and his poems, dragging their sonic weight
        like a bag of rocks from his gravely tongue
to my own, a fuse of dust measuring the way.
    They settle just fine. They will weather
        like sandstone, wind hollowing through, grit
in the teeth. I am glad for the way the stone masons
    arrange the tiles in our little courtyard, some
        with flowers and vines, some with cartooned animals,
glad for how they shuffle and deal, trying
    an iris here, a parrot over there, shifting a sunflower
        like a sun, from south-southeast to west.
I am glad the son calls one of the tiles a spider,
    though it's clearly a crab, and sets it, as though
        after long debate, at the center of the off-kilter
checkerboard he's puzzled into place, and now
    each day I walk across this botanical mosaic,
        this bestiary of stone. And how can I not be glad

for the low stone bridge down the hill that makes me
        duck in a slight bow, giving me for a moment
            the delirium of a monk as I walk into town
for coffee, or haul a bag of garbage to the cans
        at the end of our lane. I listen to the slurred
            accents of rain and birds, knowing
that they know the transient art of stone, teaching it
        to the son and father who built, they tell me,
            more than half these walls.

ABLUTIONS

If it's true as I once read it was
that while washing my hands
in the bathroom sink of the public library
some small percentage of the skin cells
on my hands went swirling—
was it clock- or counter-clockwise?—
down the ceramic vortex—maybe
sixty or seventy million of the little darlings
and that the earth's water cycle insists
that every molecule-laden micro-drop
of water stays in the glistening loop—
precipitation, evaporation, condensation,
& so on—then the man I passed bent over
& slurping from the fountain
back by the reference stacks must have been
ingesting some miniscule but no doubt
measurable percentage of my body,
unaware I'd just been rinsing soap scum with water
transubstantiated with the cells of whatever
the old reference librarian had for lunch
& sighed into the toilet as she peed—was it
cream of broccoli soup? tuna & swiss on rye?
& maybe—I want to think—a sip of brandy
from a monogrammed flask she dug from her hefty purse—
& my hands still gliding around each other
unbeknownst in their little mobius romp.
I have no evidence for any of this,
only some circumstantial residue I finger-flick away
as the hand-dryer discharges recombinant
molecules of air onto my hands—the same

ball-throwing, fly-swatting, crotch-jostling hands
that sometimes shade my eyes from too much sun—
some things are hard to see—& we are brethren
& lovers then—part & particle as Emerson wrote
of one another, co-conspirators—think vaporous
linkages of breath—parent & child, predator & prey
of each other's cells, devouring & devoured
but also—& this would be essential
to the helixing hypothesis—oblivious
as we pass each other in the stacks, or pry
from our wallets the bar-coded identities
that allow us when we finally make it
to the circulation desk to check out
our allotment of fashion magazines &
New Arrival DVDs before turning for the door
& going as we all will go on our way.

SLASH & BURN

I've heard about the eye
in the ozone hole, the heavens'
infrared glare siphoning up
the secular detritus of our glee.

It's like the tailings of light
kited behind the chimney swifts
as they lasso themselves
down the abandoned smokestack
at dusk. Blink, and then blink.

Or the hair-line of the horizon
limning the border between ocean and sky,
desert and spired city, noosing itself
like the self-consuming snake
of hieroglyphic lore, until it too
becomes pin-prick small, winking out
like a vacuum-tubed television
signing off.

I can feel the burn
on the back of my neck,
a mid-life stippling, as I fling
another branch onto
the brush pile—maple bough
and oak limb, armloads
of spindly ash—as I pitch in
the kerosened torch.

So much depends
on conflagration, on spark.
So much fire, so much quelling
of originary noise.

Small animals peer in
at the withered edge of the fire,
primed by mythic hungers—

while smoke frays
through the armature
of the trees, ribbons of syntax
hollowing to echo.

LETTER FROM SOUTHERN CALIFORNIA

They're tearing down the store where, years ago, I watched
a floof-haired woman with (*how to say this in a poem?*) astonishing breasts

clack to her red convertible in a black halter top,
gold-glitter lettering splayed across the front: "They're Real."

Oh, I suppose they were and it was, then, coastal California,
opulent and loaded with reality, sun slamming onto breakers,

dump trucks hauling four-ton boulders to hold back
the sea's assault on real estate, that swell of climactic greed,

sea-walls piled in front of five-million dollar second homes,
giving it all an air-brushed feeling of permanence.

Only a few dozen hillsides and gullies gave way
to last month's rains, the mountains shorn by the last round

of wildfires, inclines chewed by rivulets churning to rivers
as chaparral roots unlatched, let go. They say you can see it

from outer space, or pull it up on Google Earth, click on
the "Street Level" view option, and there you are, or here, standing

where I am, on a stuccoed veranda, the rain gone back
where it belongs, watching a Mexican worker go over a driveway

one more time with a Shop-Vac. Lord, the Good Samaritans of L.A.
are drawing up spreadsheets with DreamWorks executives

and corporate tycoons to streamline the donation of uneaten
banquet spreads for food pantries and shelters. I heard it on NPR

this morning as I sliced a banana into my steel-cut oatmeal,
sprinkled half a teaspoon of raw, unbleached sugar across

the steaming bowl. There was a story about Jimmy Carter's
new children's book, and one about the seven-billionth person

recently born unto this fair blue planet. I felt good
about the world right then, about America and Woody Guthrie songs

and the woman with the ad-campaign sequined across her chest.
The sun was going all kaleidoscopic across the waves, like I was

living in that pop-art Matisse cartoon of the circling dancers,
all of us naked and catching fire as we swayed.

PRAYER FOR MY DAUGHTERS IN THE ANTHROPOCENE

If I take the trees at their invariably varying word, which,
even threadbare and silent, I do, I know that the rivers of voltage

fluming through the sky, pouring from cloudbank to wind shoal,
and sparking invisibly at the nodules and nodes of branch tips

plunge deep into the microfibered network below the roots,
wash through the thickets of fungus and mold, and hum the day.

And I know that the ants and snails and the million tiny leapers
in their constant migration from dirt to trunk, trunk to dirt, dirt

to grass blade and loam knot and weathering stone, carry with them
some trace of the everywhere they've been, and leave behind

a whisper-thin thread that spiders could envy, an eons-old map
drawn with dust motes on a panel of wind. Which is why, even now,

when they are mostly grown, maybe too rooted for such
retro-wishes, I wish my daughters back up into the branches

of linden and maple, poplar and spruce, the high trees
they inhabited when they, both daughters and trees, were younger.

Back up into the swaying solidity of carbon, where they chattered
and dreamed, scraped shins and bled a little into the indifferent
    circuitry of wood.

Despite appearances, this father's wish is anti-nostalgic, pinioned
    as it is
to chaos and entropy, the way up full of promise the way down

can't foresee. Why I wish them plugged into that vast array, wired
to the real, and thereby unplugged from the hundred gadgets,

the shiny blinders, the vortexing algorithms of modern life, wish them
high enough up the arboreal fretwork for view to become vision,
   teetering

above the grass like drunken parrots, bright-eyed mystics of leaf
and bud and floating seed, clinging and clung to, and all of a piece.

Another Dream in Which

the ridge lines and cirques,
the streams and alpine meadows spill down
from their unaccountable heights
into the city.

I like where I am well enough:
robins hunting the obedient lawn,
squirrels circumnavigating the yard
by power lines.

But the dream has me on the rooftop
of the red brick building alongside the other
red brick buildings, the street noise
murmuring up like creek water
twelve stories below.

I should look more often up into
the sky above the roofs and water towers,
the daubs of cloud, the commas
of gray-black paint
that might become birds.

A staircase at one corner
of the tar-black roof climbs
a steep expanse, vanishing into lilac or
rhododendron—the dream is
botanically imprecise.

Later I'll realize that the granite-
block stairs are an outtake
from a gorge in Maine I hiked
forty years before. The dream, as always,
plagiarizes the life.

But that is a different dream
from this, another kind of distance—
though in both I stay put, legs fevered
to the floor, sentenced to another night
of peering through a gap in the stars,
the stairs bending into a tangle of green
I can't see from here.

Perseids Meteor Shower

I wasn't thinking of heaven
when I set the alarm for 3 A.M., but of how
summer deepens like a thought,
and what I wanted was to drift along that swell,
and so rose or more like staggered
out of bed and padded through the cool grass,
laying myself down on the small dock
on the small pond fringed with its
inscrutable reeds, and stared up into the swales,
ready for the stars I'd been told would
streak past by the dozens, fragments of worlds
blazing out through the cricket-plumed night.
And like many oceanic dreamers,
I fell asleep. And like most I woke
to the singed core of night, and lay there,
stilled beneath the expanse, until I made out
not the streaks of promised stellar dust,
but the quick charcoaled arcs of bats
hunting above the little pond. Four of them,
seven, maybe a dozen swooped and
curled above my outpost, silent as stars,
dark as the space between. I tried to follow
the zithering blurs, those ingenious,
inverted stars plotting brief constellations
against the dark. I thought of a closer heaven,
as I peered over the edge of the visible.

ONE BRIDGE, ONE WHISKEY, ONE MOON

And two men leaning
on the riveted steel,
        paying no attention

        to the moon, the same one,
they know well enough,
        that took poor Li Po

        by the hand, and led him
that summer night deep
        into his river's delirious curl.

        Two men, as the songs
will have it, tipping
        plastic cups of whiskey,

        talking, as poets do,
the fiddle-dee-dee of poems:
        the canal's slurred cadence,

        the darkened calligraphy
of the town. No one hears
        what their words ignite.

        No one sees the tiny bells
of smoke purling away from
        their mouths.

        And as they talk, the moon drops
over and over into the current,
        shattering, as moons do,

a thousand years of poems.

FOUR

Mid-Life Asceticism

I've given up the star chart
of my father's death,
that fading constellation, but not
the moon of my mother's,
gibbous and silver in the sky.

I've given up the ratcheting chorus
of tree frogs crooning the day
to a close, but not the idling pulse of crickets
churning the summer grass awake.

I've given up piling stones on the earth
to leave some sign of my passing,
though sometimes, when no one
is watching, I toss sticks behind me as I go,
a trail to follow back, a game
to tire the hungry dogs.

I've given up my hands
down my pants, watching Grace Kelly
hail a cab on 7th Avenue, but not
Kate Hepburn swirling kiss-colored
burgundy in a long-stemmed glass
on her father's front porch.

I've sworn off Rembrandt's light,
but not Vermeer's, and turned away from
Picasso's scissors, though not Matisse's.
As for the Brueghels, I've given up one
but kept the other, though I'd rather not say
which is the father, which the son.

I've abandoned phone calls and emails,
faxes and telegrams, but not
sweet gossip passed across the fence,
and not Post-its or shopping lists—
clues to remind me the way home every night.

As for sorrow and anger, I've booted
those hothouse blossoms halfway down
the basement steps, but I've held tight
to love, the anchorite's anchor, that deep
clarifying drink, even though some days
my mouth comes away from that cup
thirsting for things that linger
at the tip of my tongue.

All this in less than a month
of sitting in a damp antiluvial cave,
a rock for a pillow, fistfuls of sand
to rub into my hair. All this,
as the years come knocking,
and the songs drift away, and the dust
swirls importantly each time
I go to the door.

Some Ants for Henry Thoreau

It wasn't the light this morning, edgy as it was.
  And it wasn't the air the light edged through, dazzling
if familiar, churning with the scent of new leaves.
  It wasn't even three or four other things
that it might have been, most of them nondescript
  little ruins, tiny brilliances. . . . It was the dumb luck
of my daughter leaving half a plastic Easter egg
  on the front walk, a green one, inside of which
was a smaller, chocolate egg. Peering close,
  I watched as several hundred pin-pointed ants,
the color of willow bark or rained-on dirt,
  swarmed the pink enamel like a universe of mouths.
I know it's spring on the Merrimack, and I know
  in a few weeks I'll begin each day by tracing back
along a line of ants, starting at the kitchen sink,
  (some coffee grounds, crumbs swept from the bread board),
then moving to the window sill, out
  through an invisible crack, to the red brick just starting
to gather warmth, down to the flagstones,
  tracking the cord of them—insatiable! unrepentant!—
and on toward the birdbath, the interwoven
  hedge, the meadow where the cows nod
their quiet assent. And then I lose them, Henry,
  as I always do, in the uncut thistly weeds near the barn.
To begin each day among the weeds, crouched
  and hungry for a sign of complete desire, this
is my small prayer. To pull a blade of grass and watch
  a single globe of dew fade and blink out.
To follow the notes of a disappearing bird
  out into the trees, up and out along the farthest

branch, laying my fingers against the pulse
    of that blue-fletched, warbling throat.
Such moments can kill a man, or startle him back
    to his senses. It is Easter, my friend, and you are
a long time cold beneath the thawed Concord dirt. I am sorry
    to be so long in writing. Winter has been hard
on all of us here, taking half the trees in the orchard,
    pinning us close to the warmth of mostly human fires.
But the ants have returned to urge us back out,
    carrying the great, sloughed-off fragments of the world
from one place to another. They are your ants,
    dear Henry, always circling for the center,
always gnawing, always pushing, always calling us
    to bend close to their crafty, diligent shows.

For My 11th Grade English Teacher, Who Gave Me a Book of Ryōkan's Poetry

I underlined *Daigu*, Great Fool,
the name the poet took
not long before his father threw himself,
heavy as a sack of grain, into the roils
of the Katsura River.

I circled *Gogō-an*, his hermitage-hut
clamped like a knot of lichen
to the side of Mt. Kugami, the place he named
after five measures of rice.

At sixteen, everything was a sign:
—the game of looping grass,
—the game of matching stones,
—the game of pulling from the sleeves of my robe
woven balls of colored silk, showing
the village children the secret of the bouncing art:
one, two, three, four, five, six, seven.

How easy in that sputtering decade
of Saigon's fall and Disco's rise
to glimpse myself in the gaps
between Tokugawan Japanese and late-
Nixonian English. How simple
to lose myself in the artless art
of a hermit-monk-poet, the quick-witted,
moon-spooning Zen-wino,
playing dead by the side of the road.

And you, Mrs. Wilchek, who was it
you glimpsed hiding among the peach blossoms
on the hill, sitting cross-legged
by the spoiled waters of the Potomac?
I held out my begging bowl
and you tossed in a word.

CHAOS THEORY

The wind returns
to pick up where it started,
  the where and what. The weather, too, turns,
turns into what it wants—

  its own desire.
What and whom. The how and
  howl of roofs peeled from walls like
orange rind, of walls snipped

  and gaped, socketed
like eyes, of trees unscrewed
  from their latches, a thousand
frayed threads tossed like words

  by babbling tongues,
syllables snatched from open mouths,
  cries whipped away like headlong
funneling water, cataracts inverted,

  the who and hurl
of gravity unstrung from bedrock motivations,
  couch cushions, bowling trophies,
delta-loamed blues records

  moaning and spun,
a mail sack billowed with nobody's mail,
  lawn edgers, jumper cables, the jump-drive
hardwired hyper-jazz

of upended skies,
the uncoupled train-wreck wind that is,
        it whispers, every rooted thing's
    desire, the center's

                unwobbling core,
the only *what* that lasts, the only
        where on which
    this dirt-flecked grappling stand can be made.

INFINITIVES

To know what the crows know,
juggling noises at the top of a snag.

To love the wind that much,
face-forward into all that syntax.

To rhyme the rivaling verbs *crave* and *slake*,
and follow their music as far as it goes.

To gather back to yourself a few insignificances,
glanced-over trifles and wished-for particulars,

that may well be, as you've been told,
better off unheeded, better left to their ordinary

undersung selves, except that they are yours,
and the day feels ample enough for their telling.

To tramp the surging streets of the city,
slowing for bakeries and sleight-of-handers,

for spare-changers and string trios, reeling in
the Michelangelos of sidewalk chalk,

the Lorcas of postcard poetry—
a dollar a sonnet, quatrains only a quarter.

To settle into a game of firebrand chess
with a Polish émigré in Washington

Square Park, or, in Washington Heights,
to a lazy game of checkers with the gray-eyed

daughter of a Dominican shopkeeper,
even though the fix is in, the chips are down,

even though the man selling shaved ice on the corner
eyes you knowingly, raising the stakes.

To edge close enough to the world
you can hear the hornets chewing

through the trees, consecrating
with their spit those vast papery hives.

To watch the unending line of ants
disassemble the world, grain by magnificent grain

in one place, and then, grain by grain,
piece it back together somewhere else.

To slip outside in your bare feet and bathrobe,
and press your ear to the ground—

grass or gravel, sun-struck or sleeted,
it doesn't matter. To listen to what the earth insists,

renew, renew—though its voice, after so much
human noise, has gone thin and raspy.

To hear what the locksmith or the jewel thief hears
as the tumblers slide into place.

To soot up your face, and pull down
your watch-cap. To snip through the wire fence

and set free the eight-hundred mink
from the North Dakota mink farm.

To hunch under the hemlocks as those
shimmering bodies pour back into the trees,

the planet tipped again toward wildness,
less desiccated a moment, less drained.

To apologize to the industrialist's wife
as you slip through the unlocked

patio door and blindfold and cart off
her silk-suited husband. To haul him

through the manicured hedges of his yard
and bundle him into the unmarked van.

To lend him a pillow and feed him well, but still
to jostle him onto the waiting plane,

then shoulder him into the idling taxi.
To hold him steady, rumpled and open-eyed,

before the sweatshop, oil slick, denuded
forest, chemical stew—to see that he sees

in the far-flung eddies and hovels of the world
the flourishing havoc of his greed.

To give the grasses back to the prairies
and the prairies to the bison.

To give the bison back to the wolves,
and the wolves to the edge of their hunger.

To see what the farmer sees as he walks
his father's and his grandfather's farm,

the stories of the land dug in and rooted,
conjuring back their resilient fruit.

To know the weight of hay piled
on the tines of a pitchfork, and then

the weight released as you swing it up
and into the back of a '68 Dodge

rattling across the field. To mark
a clear distinction between myth and truth.

To walk when you can, and run when
you have to. To use more pepper,

less salt. To drink less, but when you drink,
to drink better—Zinfandel in January,

Sauvignon Blanc in June, washing
the day down with cold quaffs of water.

To learn to juggle plums and apples,
so the air is sluiced with color,

the day grown tipsy as a county fair.
To tell time by the interlapping tongues

of sun and shadow—that chiaroscuric kiss,
charting the hours by the delectable

clicking of water-rattled stones.
To warm yourself at love's own fire.

To give yourself to the branches of the linden
out front, the tree, after all, consecrated

to love, that widens as it climbs, welcoming
daughters into the lift of its aerie.

To watch the woman who married you
brush her hair for the thousand-

thousandth time, humming back to herself
in the bathroom mirror. To see

what mirrors see when the room
has emptied. To know hunger

by the fuzz on the teeth, and longing,
its cousin, by what it does not say.

To kiss your way through a darkened room
of a hundred mouths, your hands

clasped behind your back, your face
tipped forward into such dark luxury,

and to know in the full blind certainty
of the body's famished Braille,

which parted lips, which tongue, which slight
quavering of breath are part of who you are.

To walk through a forest
without silencing what the forest is,

the tangle of alder and maple, the collapsing
of oak into ash, and the thousand lives

vanishing half a step ahead.
To learn the landscape's murmur:

to sit still, and to sit still, and to keep on
sitting still, until the place

where you are undulates out from you
like waves from an underwater bell.

To gather sunlight from the branches
of a Tuscan olive grove, and relight

the candles on van Gogh's straw hat.
To meet Kafka in Prague for a coffee,

or Beckett for a pint his last night in Dublin.
To ask Brother Walt about bandaging

the wounded, and Emily, his sister, about
God and bees, the crystalline fractions

of zero at the bone. To sit again at the small table
at Blues Alley, three feet from where

Bill Evans lamented through
a broken-hearted version of *Someone*

to Watch Over Me. To follow Philippe Petit
out along the wire, wherever it is strung,

stopping halfway across to read a book
or write a letter, resting a while

above the swaying world, calling
to the crazy birds by their given names.

To feel that quick constriction
of wonder, the sinews tipped with fire,

standing that first time before *Guernica*, the name
like a prayer, the word a door to a lexicon.

To sit one more time in Carnegie Hall
with your father, the half-measure of breath

just after the Berlin Philharmonic, von Karajan
conducting, has finished Mahler's Second—

the last of the chorus rising like smoke
in the rafters as the horns raise the roof.

Or to drive a final time with your mother
deep into the Rockies, the windows

all the way down, the smell
of sun-plunged pines filling the car.

To go back to before, when the music was
louder, the hands fuller of flesh.

To release into the wind the gathered
losses, decorous and famished as moths,

the way Jews toss bread in the river, in *tashlikh*,
shaking out their pockets,

or Japanese float gold-flamed paper lanterns
across the glimmer of a Nagasaki lake.

To watch as they rise and drift, these blessings.
To wish them, in their dissipating, well.

And then, at the end of the day, to walk
in the front door of your own house

just as your two daughters spring up
and hurl themselves at you, nothing held back.

To spill across the dining room table
the scraps and crumpled bits of paper

you have winnowed from the day, the ones
flurried down the street by the wind,

or those swept from the corners
of the high school courtyard, the neighborhood

store: wadded-up history papers
and chemistry notes, shopping lists

and lovelorn love poems. To smooth
each of them out, these spells and incantations,

artifacts and icons, until the small gifts
of their words, said aloud into the air,

topple toward order—*clavicle* and *driftwood*
finding each other at last, *bristle* and *sinuous*

going off to discover their own country.
To make something whole of the day's

strewn fragments, snippets of song pieced together
into these fleeting measures of your life.

ACKNOWLEDGEMENTS

My sincere thanks to the magazines, journals, and anthologies in which some of these poems first appeared, some in earlier, but still recognizable, incarnations:

32 Poems, for "One Bridge, One Whiskey, One Moon;" *American Literary Review*, for "Thaw;" *The Bakery*, for "Self-Portrait in Winter;" *Connotation Press: An Online Artifact*, for "Sleight of Hand," and "Swimming Lesson;" *Gettysburg Review*, for "Games That Crows Play" and "Infinitives;" *Green Mountains Review*, for "Either/Or;" *Indiana Review*, for "Because I Do Not Play the Cello;" *Lyric Poetry Review*, for "Look Up;" *Manchester Review*, for "After All;" *Massachusetts Review*, for "21st Century Lecture;" *Runes*, for "Apple Psalm" (first published as "Evangelical"); *Southern Review*, for "Garland of Bears" and "Reading Keats in October;" *Snake Nation Review* for "Apiarial" and "Brown Pelican, East Grand Terre Island, Louisiana, June, 2010;" and *Spiritus*, for "Great Blue." "21st Century Lecture" was awarded the Anne Halley Poetry Prize from the *Massachusetts Review*, and was reprinted in the anthologies, *Love Rise Up: Poems of Social Justice, Protest and Hope* (Benu Press, 2012) and *The Ecopoetry Anthology* (Trinity University Press, 2013). Several of these poems were published in the chapbook, *The Apple Psalms*, from Paper Lantern Press, Pittsburgh, PA.